YOUR KNOWLEDGE HAS VALUE

Michael A. Braun

Does it matter for the business world whether globalization worsens income inequality between and within nations?

GRIN Verlag

Bibliografische Information der Deutschen Nationalbibliothek:

Die Deutsche Bibliothek verzeichnet diese Publikation in der Deutschen National-
bibliografie; detaillierte bibliografische Daten sind im Internet über http://dnb.d-
nb.de/ abrufbar.

Dieses Werk sowie alle darin enthaltenen einzelnen Beiträge und Abbildungen
sind urheberrechtlich geschützt. Jede Verwertung, die nicht ausdrücklich vom
Urheberrechtsschutz zugelassen ist, bedarf der vorherigen Zustimmung des Verla-
ges. Das gilt insbesondere für Vervielfältigungen, Bearbeitungen, Übersetzungen,
Mikroverfilmungen, Auswertungen durch Datenbanken und für die Einspeicherung
und Verarbeitung in elektronische Systeme. Alle Rechte, auch die des auszugsweisen
Nachdrucks, der fotomechanischen Wiedergabe (einschließlich Mikrokopie) sowie
der Auswertung durch Datenbanken oder ähnliche Einrichtungen, vorbehalten.

Imprint:

Copyright © 2005 GRIN Verlag GmbH
Druck und Bindung: Books on Demand GmbH, Norderstedt Germany
ISBN: 978-3-640-18402-6

GRIN - Your knowledge has value

Der GRIN Verlag publiziert seit 1998 wissenschaftliche Arbeiten von Studenten, Hochschullehrern und anderen Akademikern als eBook und gedrucktes Buch. Die Verlagswebsite www.grin.com ist die ideale Plattform zur Veröffentlichung von Hausarbeiten, Abschlussarbeiten, wissenschaftlichen Aufsätzen, Dissertationen und Fachbüchern.

Visit us on the internet:

http://www.grin.com/

http://www.facebook.com/grincom

http://www.twitter.com/grin_com

Freie Universität Berlin

Hauptseminararbeit

Does it matter for the business world whether

globalization worsens income inequality

between and within nations?

Abgabetermin: Sonntag, 28. November 2005
Gesamtwortzahl: 5.920 Worte auf 19 Seiten
(plus 2.383 Worte auf 18 Seiten Anhang)

Michael A. Braun

Indexes

Table of contents

List of abbreviations

DC(s)	developed country (ies)
e.g.	exempli gratia (lat.); for example
FDI(s)	foreign direct investment(s)
GATT	General Agreement on Tariffs and Trade
GDP	Gross domestic product
HDI	Human Development Index
HDR	Human Development Report
i.e.	id est (lat.); this means
IMF	International Monetary Fund
LDC(s)	less-developed country (ies)
MNC(s)	Multinational corporation(s)
MNE(s)	Multinational enterprise(s)
NAFTA	North American Free Trade Agreement
NGO(s)	non-governmental organisation(s)
p.a.	per annum / per year
US(A)	United States (of America)
USD	US-Dollar
vs.	versus
WTO	World Trade Organization
WW I	World War I
WW II	World War II

Abstract

The essay's hypothesis is to suggest, globalization has led to increasing inequality and now matters for the business world. Therefore it describes globalization and income inequality in the context of specific business matters. To discuss and favour – or disfavour – the hypothesis, the author has divided these matters into three consecutive dimensions: the ethical, the political and the economical.

1   Introduction and academic method

The objectives of this essay are to describe the complex cause and nature of glob-alization in the context of how it affects public perceptions to the business world. Further on, it is shown why the topic is so controversial as well as what the impli-cations for broader socio-politics, in which business decisions should be made, are. Therefore some initial thoughts can be given before:

(a) The five drivers of contemporary world development are: globalization, demographics, consumerism, environmental resources and governmental regula-tion.[1] But what are their concrete consequences of globalism and capitalism?[2]

(b) About 1.5 billion people live for less then one USD a day; and about 27 mil-lion live under slavery-conditions.[3] There is a huge imbalance (e.g. of wealth etc.) between developed and undeveloped countries[4] – but also within countries.

(c) The concept of equality dates back to the US declaration of independence in 1776 as well as to the French Revolution in 1789. It defines a value, which forces all members of a certain society not to have differences between each other.

However, if one talks about the question whether it matters for business if global-ization worsens income inequality, he has to bear in mind there are actually two questions in it: (1) Has globalization really led to increasing inequality? - which is far away from being clear[5]; and (2) if so, does it matter (and how?) for the busi-ness world?[6] On this will be looked at in the following; the essay will describe both globalization and inequality, continued by a brief definition and a selection of thoughts on business matters in the context of globalization. Therefore three dimensions of it will be defined: the ethical, the political and the economical. Fi-nally a conclusion will be given on how, as it is assumed here, income inequality between and within nations due to effects of globalization matters for business.

---

[1] Laudicina (2004), pp5
[2] Blim (2005), pp4 – E.g. poor working condition: However, this can be the key to escape poverty.
[3] Blim (2005), pp1
[4] Blim (2005), pp2 – One example: The big differences in life expectancy, which is approximately twenty years longer in the western hemisphere than in the sub-Saharan area.
[5] Stiglitz (2002), pp12 - 'Globalization is potentially good, but the international institutions make it seem bad.' - Globalization has become a dominant theme in the 1990s.
[6] Since this essay is going to focus straight on the second question, the first one will be answered with 'yes' for the sake of continuity in the inequality chapter.

2   Theory of globalization

2.1   What is globalization? Definitions and meanings

There is a relatively high level of consensus about the basic definitions of what 'globalization' is. It is seen as a set of changes in societies and the global economy that result from stronger international trade, increased cultural exchange and major technological steps forward.[7] Due to cheap air travel, improved communication and the rise of computers as well as multinational corporations, theory says, globalization is a deepening, widening and speeding up of interconnectedness.[8]

However, the concept of globalization does not only tangent the business world, but its economical, political and cultural aspects[9] also play an important role in every other area of life, too. For example, there is a greater cultural exchange and more diversity, higher levels of travel and tourism but also more immigration, including the illegal one. For this reason a number of standards has been or is due to be applied globally; e.g. international standards of justice, the international criminal court and copyright / patents laws. Now the 'global public' has to cope with all challenges that do not stop at any nation-states border.[10] The reachability of former far-away parts of the world has formed, assumably, a 'global village'.

Nevertheless it is widely agreed, economical questions are most dominant to the explanation of what is seen as globalization.[11] Therefore, economically speaking, the concept of globalization describes the increase in international trade at a faster growth-rate than the world economy itself as well as the increase in international capital-flows including foreign direct investment due to lower barriers of trade, increased speed and density interdependence. I.e. it is the four different cross-border flows, namely of goods and services ('free trade'), of people (migration), of capital and of technology in a way that it creates a highly integrated market.[12]

Over all, this means there is a global policy-shift towards economic openness and more importance of international institutions – in consequence of an erosion of

---

[7] Black (2002), p197
[8] Held/McGrew (1999), pp1
[9] Wolf (2004), pp78
[10] One can think about pollution and environmental issues as well as social and ethical questions such as the spread of the capitalism – and democracy – from developed to developing nations.
[11] Globalization often is seen almost exclusively to the effects of trade liberalization and free trade.
[12] Black (2002), p197

national sovereignty. Through international agreements, organizations such as the WTO and IMF are formed to deal with the dimension of a globalized financial system and of the heavily increased influence of multinational corporations on it.

So globalization is the 'growing economic interdependence of countries world-wide through increasing volume and variety of cross-border transactions in goods and services, freer international capital flows, and more rapid and widespread diffusion of technology'.[13] Or in other words, 'globalization is no fanatical ideology, but a name for the process of integration across frontiers, of liberalizing market economies at a time of rapidly falling costs of transport and communications.'[14]

2.2 Defining globalization is controversial - Why?

As one can see, it is widely agreed what 'globalization' is; compared to this there is less agreement on its causes and disagreement about its special consequences. Is 'globalization' useful to describe the recent evolution in political economy? And even worse: Academic discussion questions whether it is real or only a myth.

For this reason, three schools of thought can be distinguished:[15] (1) the hyperglobalizers, (2) the sceptics and (3) the transformalists. The first see globalization as a clear denationalization which eventually leads to borderlessness and a global marketplace. Compared to this, the second prefer 'internationalization' together with 'regionalization'[16] rather than 'globalization' as description. They mention low statistical evidence and the fact that governments remain powerful. Whereas the third find, globalization is more or less a long-term historical process and only one driving force behind the changes that shape the modern world. Although theses explanations are various, it can be noted that those aspects that make us believe we live in a globalized world, are maybe not as established as it may seem.

2.3 Historical evolution

Some 'experts', and a number of historians describe globalization as a phenomenon of the 20th century. Nevertheless, exchange of goods between people and international travel to the most far away places are not new - both exist since ages.

---

[13] IMF (1997)
[14] Wolf (2004), pp37
[15] Held/McGrew (1999), pp1
[16] Oman (1999), pp 34 - This is the movement of two or more societies or economies towards a greater integration with the aim to pool their sovereignty to be stronger in the global market.

At about the last millennium, 'globalization' came up in the eastern hemisphere; the Indian Ocean and the South-Chinese Sea had prosperous places all over.[17] About 1000 to 1500, trade was not only important for goods, but also for the spread of religions, culture and specialised techniques. So, for centuries the Central Asian silk route was the most frequented transport way for goods by land; whereas the Indian Ocean had the most extended cargo and trade network.[18]

Since Chinese caravans and groups of ships followed the routs of this trade web, they formed therefore Asia's major role in international sea- and land-trade. Long before Europe had realised what distinctive role trade later will play in its history, the leadership in exchanging goods and culture over long distances was held by Asians. Therefore, overall it can be assumed that this was a globalized world yet.

Later – about end of 18th century – 'liberalization' in Europe started the second era of globalization. It resulted from 'laissez-faire' economic theory together with a removal of barriers against the free movement of goods. This in turn led to industrialization and specialization as well as declining of tariffs and other barriers to trade to protect own industries. States[19] who have engaged in this prospered and inequality fell as goods, capital and labour flowed more freely between nations.

However, from 1914 to 1947, a series of political and economic catastrophes reduced volume and importance of international trade flows. Globalization is said to have broken down in stages first with World War I, then collapsing with the crisis of the gold standard in the 1920s and 1930s and finally with World War II.

After this major collapses, 'globalization' firstly has been identified as a trend[20]; it is seen to have helped to significantly lower barriers of trade through international agreements[21] and negotiation rounds. And from the 1970s, the effects of this became increasingly visible, which eventually led to the Uruguay round to create the WTO. Therefore interconnectedness has expanded dramatically - and compared to

---

[17] Harbours such as Malacca in Malaysia were pulsating centres of international trade and culture.
[18] Since Islamic traders dominated this, they had the chance to spread their religion. This cultural expansion is the reason, why the Islam can be found today in the whole eastern hemisphere
[19] Such as the European heartland, its periphery and its colonies in the Americas and the Pacific.
[20] Bhalla (2002), p 4 – Some define 'globalization' narrower and date its beginning at the 1980s.
[21] Such as the General Agreement on Tariffs and Trade, which includes e.g.: the promotion of free trade of goods, the reduction or even elimination of tariffs and construction of free trade zones.

earlier times, the main difference is the high mobility of capital of what so ever kind (money, production and distribution) with the aim to get globally best results.

But is this global integration today really measurable higher than in, say, the beginning of the 20th century? One can assume 'yes', since the number of traded products is much higher, North-South trade more complex, FDI more important and portfolio investment flows larger and more complex. Due to this, today one third of world trade is company-internal and two thirds are related to MNC.

2.4 Critics: Anti-globalization

Since many years, the phenomenon 'globalization' is opportunity and pain in one: Its paradox is that while it brings unprecedented chances to all, it also gives rise to vulnerabilities and insecurities.[22] Therefore various aspects of globalization are not liked by certain public-interest activists as well as state-nationalists. For these, 'anti-globalization' is the name. However, this could lead to misunderstanding as these activists usually only oppose some parts of globalization, but not everything.

Over all, there is a range of 'anti-globalization', who claims globalization-results are not what were predicted and that involved institutions do not fight in the interests of the poor and the working class. Not surprising, the opposition is concentrated in Latin America and among the unskilled in advanced, western economies.

Also for some,[23] globalization threatens economic prosperity, social stability, environmental sustainability and even democracy. Therefore the crises in Latin America and Asia were seen as confirming that view. They also fear increasing autonomy and strength of firms could shape the political policy of nation-states.

For this reason it seems necessary to bring 'globalizer' and 'anti-globalizer' at one table. An example for such dialogue among representatives with different interests and opinions is the World Commission on the Social Dimension of Globalization. It recently released a report[24] on certain social aspects of globalization through the eyes of ordinary people and how to cope with it. Nevertheless it is not, one might or even could get the impression this report is more at the anti-globalization side.

---

[22] Laudicina (2004), pp5
[23] These are especially persons who are associated with the annual World Social Forum meetings.
[24] WCSDG (2004)

2.5 Supporter: Pro-globalization

Critics of globalization see corporations' power and perceived malevolence as bad. In reality, on can argue the problem isn't that the world's poorest citizens are exploited.[25] The problem is that they're unexploited, that is, they are omitted from the world's global economic system. Bringing more nations into the global economic framework can set the stage for world economic improvements and address the real problem, which isn't too much globalization, but not enough.

This is how supporters of globalization argue and therefore they can be called pro-globalizer; they point out that theory of comparative advantage suggests that free trade leads to a more efficient allocation of resources, with all involved benefiting. In general, they claim this leads to lower prices, more employment and output.

For some[26], globalization is a welcome development in terms of its assumed effects on growth and global poverty, political freedom and international cooperation. And as one author has stated,[27] 'I believe globalization – the removal of barriers for free trade and the closer integration of national economies – can be a force for good and that it has the potential to enrich everyone in the world, particularly the poor.', now this is proved since it has positive effects for people.[28] However, pro-globalizer argue that anti-globalizer use anecdotes to support their point of view and that worldwide statistics instead strongly support globalization.

Nevertheless it has to be mentioned that anti- and pro-globalizer of both the developed and the developing countries face many different and only some common issues. Whereas voters in developed countries are concerned about the changing nature of trade negotiations, consequences for unskilled and service workers (outsourcing) and the decline of welfare; in developing countries people fear the – allegeable – unbalanced nature of the trade negotiations, vulnerability to protectionism by richer countries and the high vulnerability to international financial crises.

---

[25] Wolf (2004), pp324
[26] This accounts especially for promoters of the – neoliberal – 'Washington Consensus'.
[27] Stiglitz (2002), pp12
[28] Petersen (2003), pp216 - See certain developing and / or transforming countries as an example.

3   Income inequalities

As the first dimension of the essay – globalization – is clear, one can look at the second one: income inequality. Because the perception of equality is often different depending on the context, it is important to define inequality. Although some say income inequality for the world as a whole is diminishing,[29] still 'the central economic issue related to globalization is that of inequality.'[30] But what does it mean? To obtain a detailed picture it is important to investigate more aspects.

Why does inequality, apart from the ethical point, matter and has globalization led to increased inequality? Both are far away from being clear. Although there is no evidence, at least for the last question, many see it as given. (This essay as well!) However, it can be argued standard of living is between North and South by time equalizing somewhere in the middle[31] and greater extremes within countries.[32]

3.1   What is income inequality?

To measure income inequality, first of all one has to define what 'income' is in fact. In this context, it is different to the common understanding: Here it is meant the sum of all goods and services[33] that one particular person receives in a period of time. And since it is very complicated to measure every income in this sense, the World Bank for example uses the living standard measurement surveys.[34]

Nevertheless there are many arguments against globalization, including increased inequality among nations. But for this, the World Bank's 2002 analysis says it is not true. This report lists 73 developing countries, including 24 countries that are globalizing and 49 that are not.[35] Those 24 countries economies grew at a rate about three percent in the 1970s, which increased to five percent in the 1990s.

Even all these countries have diverse economic resources and educational levels, still each of them prospered by increasing its integration into the global economy.

---

[29] Columbia
[30] Sen (2002), p 149
[31] The easiest explanation for this might be: why should one pay more for the same than another?
[32] Can one think of a world or countries without a middle-class?
[33] Both not necessarily money, but also fruits form own fields, public health and even education.
[34] LSMS – Surveys have been completed in most developing countries. In recent years it became an important tool for measuring and understanding poverty in developing countries.
[35] Depending on their strong increases in trade-to-GDP ratio since the 1980s.

Therefore on could assume, those countries who participate in the globalized network do better than those who, due to high tariffs and other practices, do not.

On the other side, many argue globalization clearly widens the inequality gap between states and between people within states, between the rich and the poor
within virtually all developing regions.[36] Further more, sceptics claim especially in
middle- and upper-income countries with skilled work forces, the income distribution is worsening.[37]

But how does it come that observer see changes, or not? Maybe recent changes in
global and between-country inequality are not marked and depend in part on the
conventions adopted form their measurement. Also the notion, globalization has
left more of the world's population in extreme poverty results maybe from igno-
rance or statistical manipulation.[38] In contrast, within-country inequality appears
to have risen clearly in two thirds of the analysed countries mainly because of the
policy drive towards domestic deregulation and external liberalisation.[39]

In addition, the predictions of standard theory about the inequality impact of international trade and capital flows explain more easily the changes observed during the globalisation of last century than during the last twenty years. Indeed,
most of the recent evidence on the inequality impact of globalization contradicts
the predictions of standard theory which is unable to capture the effect of other
factors such as domestic institutional weaknesses, the complexity of trade and finance in a multi-country multi-goods environment, persistent and rising protectionism in the North and the equity impact of other domestic reforms that are often introduced to facilitate the drive towards globalization.[40]

3.2   How can it be measured?

Economists have got several techniques to measure income inequality or distribution among certain members of a society. These techniques – typically categorized
as absolute or relative – are used in particular for the measurement of inequality,
or equality, of income within an economy.

---

[36] Hurrel/Woods (1999), pp12
[37] Stewart/Berry (1999), pp254
[38] Wolf (2004), pp37
[39] Corina (2003), abstract
[40] Corina (2003), p27

Absolute measures[41] define a minimal standard and then count the percentage of persons below. These methods are used for calculating the amount of poverty in a society; whereas relative income measures[42] compare the income of some individuals to the one of others. Therefore relative criteria are best for analyzing the distribution of income equality and inequality.

However, there is a lot criticism how to measure income, since it is not clear how it should be defined. Does it include capital gains, saved rents from home ownership and non-paid work within households? Therefore always the question arises whether the measurement's basic unit is individuals or households because of the pooling of income, scale effects and welfare transfers within families.

Moreover, the mentioned metrics often completely ignore specific personal effects such as: life cycle (current age)[43], risk aversion, leisure-work choice, characteristics (IQ, talent), education and training, inherited wealth, regional economic circumstances, discrimination of whatsoever kind and several market imperfections.

Even there is criticism; these measures still can help to understand certain issues. And if they are measured well, they provide a tool for inequality comparisons.

3.3 Inequality between nations …

Inequality can be proved wherever people are. Therefore one can look at individual and collective differences either on a person-/ or group-basis. However, to compare inequalities among e.g. nations, one should distinguish between average incomes and absolute incomes. For example[44], according to World Bank, between 1980 and 2000, Chinas average real incomes rose by 440 (!) percent. US average real incomes rose by only about 60%. So has China's participation in the global economy helped narrow its citizen's international income inequality? No, say globalization's opponents, noting that the absolute real income gap between the US and China during this time rose from USD 20.600 to USD 30.200 per person.

Both figures are correct. In 1980, China's standard of living was about 1/30 of the US level. With that low base, the way this gap could stay unchanged would be, if

---

[41] These include poverty line and poverty index.
[42] Such as Lorenz curve, Gini coefficient, standard deviation and percentile distributions.
[43] Since individuals usually start into their lives with no income, but a gradual increase till the time they retire, the proportion of young to old persons has a significant effect on relative inequality.
[44] Wolf (2004), pp197

Chinas economy would grew 30 times faster than the one of the US. However, if China continues to grow faster than the US, the absolute gap will eventually fall. Meanwhile, globalization's opponents may still proclaim that rich are getting richer, although the lot of them is improving faster, thanks to globalization.[45]

So in 2000, the world had the lowest level of inequality within the last 50 years[46] - and the group of developing countries grew even faster than developed countries. Further on, the years 1980 to 2000 could be seen, due to major improvements, as the best years in history of poor people.[47] However, today there are still great differences all over the world. According to the 2004 UN HDR[48], the average GDP per person was about USD 24.800 in countries with high, about USD 4.300 in countries with medium and only about USD 1.200 in countries with low human development based on the HDI[49]. But how do such differences arise?

Mainly, inequality is a measurement-question. Due to differences in technological development etc., countries reached different levels which divide the world on a paper-basis into groups. The upper[50] includes about 15 percent of the population and receives about 45 percent of the income. Whereas the lowest[51] include about 45 percent of the population but receives less than ten percent of the income.

But, what can rich countries do for poor? One idea might be providing open and unlimited access to their markets for products from poor countries can, according to the theory of comparative advantage, significantly lower inequality between rich and poor.[52] Therefore a new WTO round in Hong Kong on tariffs and barriers of trade will start, soon. But what will happen if there is no agreement?[53]

---

[45] Wolf (2004), pp197
[46] Bhalla (2002), pp1
[47] Bhalla (2002), p202
[48] The Human Development Report first appeared in 1990 and explicitly focuses on the concept of human development. It has engaged actively on the debate on how to define and measure poverty, development, gender equity and equality.
[49] The most important index involved is the human dev index, which takes health and education measures into account as well.
[50] This includes USA, Japan, Germany, France and the UK; altogether some 500 million people with over USD 11.500 income per year.
[51] Milanovic (2005a), p38 - This includes India, Indonesia and China; altogether 2.1 billion people with an income level under USD 1.000 per year.
[52] Blim (2005), p131
[53] Blim (2005), pp126 – Since influence is not distributed on the 'one person, one vote'-basis at international institutions, inequality can occur also in terms of votes at IMF, WTO etc.

The evolution of the income gap between poor and rich countries is related to convergence, which is the 'tendency for poorer countries to grow faster than richer ones and, hence, for their levels of income to converge'[54]. For this, a number of studies have tested whether, globally, per capita incomes are converging.

To date, the majority of studies find no evidence of absolute convergence, but many find evidence of conditional convergence, i.e. convergence having controlled for differences in technological and behavioural parameters. The lack of evidence of absolute convergence has led to claims that global income inequality is deteriorating. This is believed to be untrue. Most convergence studies are aimed at proving or disproving the neoclassical growth model and hence take the 'country' as the unit of measurement.

However, if inferences are being made about world income distribution the focus should be on 'people' than 'countries' to prevent China and Luxembourg, for example, receiving equal weighting in the analysis. Thus, it is found that poor peoples' incomes are growing faster than rich peoples' incomes, suggesting that global income inequality is in fact improving.[55] For this, one should look internal...

3.4 ... and within nations

Moreover, as mentioned earlier, inequality does not only appear between countries, but also within them. Due to this, one also can see a certain degree of competition between regions instead of nations.[56] As an example, even in the US the top-20 percent families held in 1998 about 91 percent (!) of all free wealth[57]; whereas the bottom-40 percent only held one![58] Over all, inequality arises due to less access to resources in the beginning[59], but is also a question of distribution of income (E.g. US again, in 1997 the top-20 percent received about 56 percent of the income; the bottom-40 percent only eleven percent.[60]).

---

[54] World Bank (1996)
[55] Cole/Neumayer (2003), pp 355
[56] E.g. in the field of taxes the Delaware-/ and in the field of environmental issues the California-effect – both are movements which affected whole industries to change – and influenced people.
[57] That is: stocks, bonds, and mutual funds etc., but without private home, cars and so on.
[58] Blim (2005), pp165
[59] Inequality also arises from the level of education.
[60] Blim (2005), pp165

Economic inequality may negatively affect social (e.g. insecurity, fight for distribution, impoverished middle class, fear for survival) and business capital (white
vs. blue collar, boycott of products, strikes), which could contribute to crime or
even revolution. One example for the effects of inequality might be China where
social disruptions of the poor have occurred over the years. Moreover, some argue
inequality reduces growth in poor countries and helps growth in rich ones.[61]

Indeed, falling inequality tends to come with falling poverty incidence. And rising
inequality appears more likely to put a brake on poverty reduction than facilitating
it. However, there is evidence of a trade-off for absolute inequality, suggesting
that those who want a lower absolute gap between the rich and the poor must in
general be willing to see lower absolute levels of living for poor people.[62]

After looking at the different definitions and points of view it can be claimed:
Over all, and although the observer's opinions differ, the majority of them suggest
globalization has led to increased inequality on the level of and within countries.
So the average inequality between rich and poor countries increased in 1990s, the
income inequality within developed countries has increased and the absolute poverty rose in 1990s in Africa, Middle East, Eastern Europe and Central Asia.

There is no doubt, globalization and regionalization can and do break down barriers, but also can break down social cohesion. Inequality slows down growth and
leads to political instability as well as to market failure.[63] However, poor people
do better, much better than the average, with globalization.[64]

Therefore, as a first conclusion, one can state globalization has led to increased
inequality on the level of and within countries. Bearing this in mind, one now can
question him in the next chapter; whether and if, how this raised income inequality matters for the business world.

---

[61] Barro (2005)
[62] Ravallion (2005)
[63] Milanovic (2005a), pp154
[64] Bhalla (2002), p201

4   Business matters

As defined in the beginning, the objective of this essay is to describe the complex cause and nature of globalization in the context of how it affects public perceptions to the business world. For this, it firstly was looked at what the positive and negative effects of globalization are. Continued by the finding globalization dramatically has changed the context in which global businesses interact.

No doubt, globalization's 'widening, deepening and speeding up of worldwide interconnectness'[65] truly has a great impact on the business world in a 'completely new epoch of human history where people are increasingly subject to the one and only global market place with ever stronger global mechanisms of governance.'[66]

But how does globalization affect businesses in terms of inequality as questioned? What are the concrete, vital business matters? Or in other words, what do firms want – or need to do? What are the impacts on corporate governance and organization? Firms need to understand how globalization's positive/negative consequences fundamentally altered the context in which business decisions are made.

Therefore it seems to be best firstly to distinguish between the three dimensions in which the business world interacts: the social/ethical, the political and the economical dimension – and later to put them together again. Through this, consequences and implications for the business world as well as answers to the question of who is part of that 'game' can be and will be found.

4.1   Ethical dimension

Technology[67] and the media enabled people to get access to information on different income levels, working conditions as well as supply and demand in the world. This makes comparisms of living standards (and its divergences!) more obvious than in former times. Following the concept of equality (every citizen has the equal 'value' as everyone else) as mentioned before, this inevitably leads to criticism of MNEs e.g. paying different wages for a certain kind or type of work in different countries or continents and a rising demand for political consequences.

---

[65] Held/McGrew (1999), pp1
[66] Held/McGrew (1999), pp 1-21
[67] Singh / Dhumale (2004), pp145 - Nevertheless, some argue the support of the modern information technology in the current stage of globalization is not measurable more than other factors. However, the full potential of this is not seen as being fully realized in the developing world.

So, one can argue for the urgent importance of social peace and social stability, which is a major factor if it comes to the decision either for or against a production plant location etc. However, this stability and security is endangered through inequality either within or between nations. Therefore, globalization has forced – and forces – companies to tackle social and ethical problems on a global basis.

4.2 Political dimension

Apart from the ethical – or unethical – point of view, inequality also leads to higher government spending, which in turn weakens states additionally. If limited public resources need to be spended in smoothening inequality. On the other side there is no money left for other important things. In terms of the business world this might be a good infrastructure, sound education and purchasing power etc. Further on, inequality within countries (but also between) leads to a consumption short back, which again, does weaken both the business world and the states.

The HDR 2005 was intended to bring this very problem of (income) inequality among other social problems to the minds of state representatives just before the (Millennium +5) summit.[68] The increased pressure from NGOs could lead to international action that addresses both global poverty and global inequality.[69] [70]

A legal framework and stabilizing mechanisms to reduce trade barriers, improve market access and enhance international trade while stabilizing the monetary system where needed to support global economic growth and the closely correlated poverty reduction by global governance through international organisations such as WTO, IMF and World Bank has been set.[71] Also it aims to preserve intellectual property rights and provide developing countries with special support to improve their competitiveness in the global market place.

The emphasis of this report lies on the growing problems which arise from income inequality within and between countries. According to this, only the correction of unequal access to (re-)sources and the distribution of power within and be-

---

[68] FES (2005)
[69] Milanovic (2005b), p9
[70] International action could lead to a global redistribution of income through taxes that could be raised from businesses in developed countries by an international body as the shift of power from nation states to NGOs in certain areas might allow for a special global tax agency in the future.
[71] World Bank (2005)

tween countries ultimately could produce a continuous and vital progress in human development. The increasing pressure from NGOs could lead to international action that addresses both global poverty and global inequality[72]

However, not only inequality, but different types of political risk are also major challenges for the business world in times of globalization. If companies are engaging in foreign countries either producing- and/or selling-wise, they might face political risks like such: (1) expropriation, nationalisation and confiscation of production plants and valuables, (2) de facto expropriation, (3) currency risk, (4) risk of political violence and (5) breach of contract and sanctions.[73] But in terms of inequality only some seem to be relevant: Namely the forth one deals with the classic kind of risk that affects inequality and the underlying entrepreneurial decisions. Because war, civil war, revolution, terrorism, sabotage or movements towards independence often arise for inequality reasons, they should be mentioned.

As an even more recent development, new sources of risk (in the broader sense) for companies came up: pressure of NGO's against globalization (see chapter on anti-globalization) together with major disruptions, strong internationally organised crime and corruption. Especially the last one – together with bribery – comes up with greater inequality in the world as shown in the transparency index. Further on, political disruptions and riots can arise somewhere and spread from on to another country like a fire in the wind with the result of worsened inequality.

4.3 Economical dimension

The demand, however, for a more equal access to resources and potential changes in policies[74] could reduce the net earnings of businesses by diminishing the comparative cost advantages of the current lower cost production in developing countries. Therefore changes of the ethical/social and political dimension could affect the business world to a certain degree. Also the potential reduction of disposable income of the consumers in developed countries requires a more global thinking of the distribution of future wealth and markets.

---

[72] Milanovic (2005b), p9
[73] Moran (1999), pp15
[74] Such as the yet mentioned taxes for global income redistribution from businesses / consumers.

However, also the globally ever more growing income inequality has an impact on the business world already: traditional chains of production, marketing and delivery do not exist any more[75] and within developed countries greater income disparities mainly result from the loss (or move) of less-qualified jobs in the production-/ and service-sector towards countries, which have lower costs – with strong consequences to the global market place with its diverse actors ...

In the U.S. for example, the 20 million American families who are classified as working poor, 'now run the risks of seeing their incomes slashed by half in any given year'. That is nearly double the volatility of the middle income families.[76]

However, in general 'the emergence of global production systems that were imposed by the massive sums of FDI has created new opportunities for growth and industrialization in developing countries.'[77] About 65.000 MNEs with some 850.000 foreign affiliates are the drivers behind the global production systems. They now coordinate the huge global supply chains which link firms across.

Whereas the growth of these global production chains has been most prominent in the high tech industries (electronics, semi-conductors, etc.) and in labour intensive consumer goods (textiles, garments and footwear), it now became significant in the service sector, too. In this area, technological advances have made it more than possible for services such as software development, financial services and call centres to be supplied from different countries all around the world.[78]

For labour intensive consumer goods, MNEs design the product, specify the quality etc., and then outsource its production to cheap, local firms in developing countries. They exercise control over the quality and timing of production, which is often subject to changes in design and volume. The driving force is the flexible and timely adjustment to changes in consumer demand with minimal inventory cost. The MNEs also control the marketing of the product with own brandings.

---

[75] Importer – Exporter, Multinationals and common structure provider.
[76] Gosselin (2004) – Most of theses families have got already a second or third job, yet.
[77] Carr/Chen (2003)
[78] Lall (2004) – One can think especially of India where all these services are offered.

The governance structure of the global financial system[79] has also been transformed. As private financial flows have come to dwarf official flows, the role and influence of private actors such as banks, hedge funds, equity funds and rating agencies has increased substantially. As a result these private financial agencies now exert tremendous economic power over the economic policies of developing countries, especially the emerging market economies, and the business world.

The increased influence of private actors in the global financial system initially should have led to greater efficiency in worldwide allocation of resources as well as to the associated benefit of exerting greater, and much needed, market discipline on developing country governments. The combined effect of these developments in trade, FDI, finance and technology has had a profound and varying impact on economic sectors, enterprises, categories of workers and social groups.

Expanding global markets for goods and services provided new outlets for the exports of industrial countries while the emergence of global production systems and liberalized investment rules generated new opportunities for their MNEs, increasing their global reach and market power.

To bring it together, the phenomenon of globalization and (the growing) income inequality does offer not only challenges to the business world, but also great possibilities.[80] There are new targets for the distribution of own products, a far broader HR potential, a (assumably) better cost structure as well as chances in logistics and transport. Compared to this, the reputation risk, direct and indirect negative influences on company profits, a (maybe) changed motivation of the working force and political restrictions are side effects which can be managed.

As shown, the three dimensions in which the businesses interact – ethical, political and economical – are going together hand in hand and build on each other from an overview to a more focused point of view. Moreover, there is two outside dimensions: the first, which is the moralist-ethical and the public-political dimension and the second one which is more internal (basically profits) oriented.

---

[79] And even the approach of how to cope with problems, corporate governance, either in the Anglo-Saxon or in the more European-Japanese way, has changed.
[80] One can think of the Coase theorem which focuses on the presence of side effects (externalities).

5   Results and conclusion

As stated previously, the objectives of this essay were to describe how public perceptions to the business world work in the context of globalization and what the implications for broader socio-politics, in which decisions are made, are.[81]

Therefore, straight away, a conclusion of whether it matters for the business world that globalization worsens the income inequality between and within nations, is that worsening income inequality through globalization on both levels definitely has severe impacts to businesses, i.e. it matters. But how and why?

According to the three dimensions[82] in which businesses have to interact in the globalized world, the growing income inequality produces consumer demand shifts in the services and goods markets. Businesses now have to adapt to these changes in order not to loose profits, customers and market share. Also it might incur political risks, as mentioned, such as expropriation in poorer countries.

Moreover, stronger ethical and political pressure will let the private sector realize that it is to their self-interest to support 'some form of global action to deal with both poverty and inequality.'[83] Further on, the business world will have to rethink their policies, if they want to remain competitive in the future. Some of them certainly have, but potentially more dramatic increases in bankruptcies of businesses that will not follow the fast track of globalization might be seen.

In a more general sense, one could conclude the essay as well in another direction: Inequality is, as proofed above, harmful to the business world in different senses. And equality and stability of the society are public goods to all. Unfortunately there are some individual actors that do 'free riding'[84] for the sake of short term profits such as violating standards of equality and fair treatment. This in turn leads to the classical 'tragedy of the commons'[85], which illustrates the conflict for re-

---

[81] Not to forget, the essay actually consisted of two questions: (1) Has globalization led to increasing inequality? - which is not clear to all; and (2) if so, (how) does it matter for the business world?
[82] As defined: the ethical, the political and the economical dimension of business matters.
[83] Milanovic (2005a)
[84] This are actors that take more than their fair share or do not burden the cost of their specific use.
[85] Hardin (1968)

sources[86] between the interests of individuals (e.g. one specific company or a certain industry) vs. the common public (e.g. population, employees etc.).

Moreover, this tragedy of the business world vs. the society can be seen as a collective prisoner's dilemma. Imagine a specific company has two options: either it could cooperate with all other participants in the 'game' or defect from them. Cooperation is when the organisation agrees to protect the commons (equality standards etc.) to avoid the tragedy (i.e. riots, boycotts, etc.).

However, there is no doubt that the world has a chance to work together in a more constructive and fair way. 'If history teaches anything, it is that we have choices. We can choose a better world – or a worse one.'[87] Therefore one only has to grab this choice and get the best out of it. And the world needs more globalization, not a reduced one, to raise its collective standard of living.[88]

And, 'if globalization continues to be conducted in the way that it has been in the past, if we continue to fail to learn from our mistakes, globalization will not only not succeed in promoting development but will continue to create poverty and instability.'[89] Is this really what we want? Probably not ...[90]

---

[86] This concept primarily was concerned with human population growth and farm land; it now is focused on the use of the atmosphere and oceans etc. – such as mentioned above – as well.
[87] Wolf (2004), pp24
[88] Wolf (2004), pp49
[89] Stiglitz (2002), pp12
[90] However, this would raise far more new questions to the essay such as how to prevent poverty in the future and to lift up certain parts of the world's population onto a different standard of living. In addition one could question as well, how a certain power-state which preserves regulatory autonomy vs. a trade nation which rather prefers to build up international organisations engages in this field.

Appendixes

List of references

Barro (2000): Barro, R., *Inequality and Growth in a Panel of Countries*, Journal of Economic
Growth, [Internet 21.10.2005]:
www.post.economics.harvard.edu/faculty/barro/papers/p_inequalitygrw.pdf

Bhalla (2002): Bhalla, S., *Imagine there is no country – Poverty, inequality and growth in the era
of globalization*, Institute for international economics, Washington, 2002

Black (2002): Black, J., *Dictionary of Economics – An indispensable source of reference covering
over 2.500 terms*, 2nd edition, Oxford University Press, Oxford, 2002

Blim (2005): Blim, M., *Equality and economy – the global challenge*, AltaMira Press, Walnut
Creek, 2005

Carr/Chen (2003): Carr, M. / Chen, M., *Globalization, social exclusion and work: with special
reference to informal employment and gender*, background paper for the World Commission, Geneva, 2003. Cited in: World Commission on the Social Dimension of Globalization, A Fair Globalization: Creating Opportunities for all, Geneva, 2004.

Cole/Neumayer (2003): Cole, M. / Neumayer, E., *The pitfalls of convergence analysis: is the income gap really widening?*, Applied Economics, vol. 10, 06-03, [Internet 21.10.2005]:
http://www.econpapers.repec.org/article/tafapeclt/v_3A10_3Ay_3A2003_3Ai_3A6_3A
p_3A355-357.htm

Columbia: Columbia University, [Internet 21.10.2005]:
http://www.columbia.edu/~xs23/papers/worldistribution/NYT_november27.htm

Corina (2003): Corina, G., *The impact of liberalisation and globalisation on income inequality in
developing and transitional economies*, CES-ifo working paper No. 843, Florence, 2003

FES (2005): Friedrich-Ebert-Stiftung, *Briefing Papers*, 10/2005, Berlin, 2005

Gabler (2003): (o.V.), *Gabler Kompakt-Lexikon Volkswirtschaft – 3.500 Begriffe nachschlagen,
verstehen, anwenden*, 2. Auflage, Gabler, Wiesbaden 2003

Hardin (1968): Hardin, G., *The Tragedy of the Commons*, Science [Internet 25.10.2005]:
http://www.sciencemag.org/sciext/sotp/commons.dtl

Held/McGrew (1999): Held, D. / McGrew, A., *Global Transformations - Politics, Economics and
Culture*, Polity Press, Cambridge, 1999

Hurrel/Woods (1999): Hurrel, A. / Woods, N. (ed.), *Inequality, globalization and world politics*,
Oxford University Press, Oxford, 1999

IMF (1997): International Monetary Fund, *World Economic Outlook*, 05/97, Washington, 1997

Lall (2004): Lall, S., *The employment impact of globalization in developing countries*, ILO mimeo, Geneva, 2002, cited in: World Commission on the Social Dimension of Globalization, A Fair Globalization: Creating Opportunities for all, Geneva, 2004

Laudicina (2004): Laudicina, P., *World out of balance*, McGraw-Hill, New York, 2004

LSMS: World Bank, *Living Standard Measurement Surveys*, Washington, [Internet 21.10.2005]: www.worldbank.org/lsms/

Milanovic (2005a): Milanovic, B., *Worlds apart – Measuring international and global inequality*, Princeton University Press, Princeton, 2005

Milanovic (2005b): Milanovic, B., *Both global poverty and global inequality must be addressed*, 28 October 2005, Taipei Times, Taipei, 2005

Moran (1999): Moran, T., *Managing international political risk*, Longman, Harlow, 1999

Petersen (2003): Petersen, H., *Globalisierung und soziale Gerechtigkeit*, in: Reitz, S. (ed.), Theoretische und wirtschaftspolitische Aspekte der internationalen Integration – Festschrift für Helga Luckenbach zum 68. Geburtstag, Duncker & Humblot, Berlin, 2003

Oman (1999); Oman, C., *Defining Globalization*, in: Hurrel, A. / Woods, N. (ed.), Inequality, globalization and world politics, Oxford University Press, Oxford, 1999

Ravallion (2005): Ravallion, M., *A poverty-inequality trade-off?*, World Bank, Policy Research Working Paper no. WPS 3579, 05/05, [Internet 21.10.2005]: http://www.econ.worldbank.org/external/default/main?pagePK=64165259&theSitePK= 469372&piPK=64165421&menuPK=64166093&entityID=000012009200505051 34719

Sen (2002): Sen, A., citied in: Milanovic, B., *Worlds apart – Measuring international and global inequality*, Princeton University Press, Princeton, 2005

Singh / Dhumale (2004): Singh, A., / Dhumale, R., *Globalization, technology and income inequality – a critical analysis*, in: Inequality, growth and poverty in an era of liberalization and globalization, Oxford University Press, Oxford, 2004

Stewart/Berry (1999); Stewart, F. / Berry, A., *Defining Inequality*, in: Hurrel, A. / Woods, N. (ed.), Inequality, globalization and world politics, Oxford University Press, Oxford, 1999

Stiglitz (2002): Stiglitz, J., *Globalization and its discontents*, W.W. Norton, New York, 2002

WCSDG (2004): World Commission on the Social Dimension of Globalization, *A Fair Globalization: Creating Opportunities for All*, February 2004, [Internet 21.10.2005]: http://www.ilo.org/public/english/fairglobalization/index.htm

Wolf (2004): Wolf, M., *Why globalization works*, Yale University Press, Cambridge, 2004

World Bank (1996): World Bank, *Forget Convergence: Divergence Past, Present, and Future*, 09 June 1996, [Internet 21.10.2005]: www.worldbank.org/fandd/english/0696/articles/090696.htm

List of countries ranked by the Human Development Index 2005

Rank	Country	HDI
High human development		
1	Norway	0.963
2	Iceland	0.956
3	Australia	0.955
4	Luxembourg	0.949
5	Canada	0.949
6	Sweden	0.949
7	Switzerland	0.947
8	Republic of Ireland	0.946
9	Belgium	0.945
10	United States	0.944
11	Japan	0.943
12	Netherlands	0.943
13	Finland	0.941
14	Denmark	0.941
15	United Kingdom	0.939
16	France	0.938
17	Austria	0.936
18	Italy	0.934
19	New Zealand	0.933
20	Germany	0.930
21	Spain	0.928
22	Hong Kong	0.916
23	Israel	0.915
24	Greece	0.912
25	Singapore	0.907

26	Slovenia	0.904
27	Portugal	0.904
28	South Korea	0.901
29	Cyprus	0.891
30	Barbados	0.878
31	Czech Republic	0.874
32	Malta	0.867
33	Brunei Darussalam	0.866
34	Argentina	0.863
35	Hungary	0.862
36	Poland	0.858
37	Chile	0.854
38	Estonia	0.853
39	Lithuania	0.852
40	Qatar	0.849
41	United Arab Emirates	0.849
42	Slovakia	0.849
43	Bahrain	0.846
44	Kuwait	0.844
45	Croatia	0.841
46	Uruguay	0.840
47	Costa Rica	0.838
48	Latvia	0.836
49	Saint Kitts and Nevis	0.834
50	Bahamas	0.832
51	Seychelles	0.821
52	Cuba	0.817
53	Mexico	0.814

54	Tonga	0.810
55	Bulgaria	0.808
56	Panama	0.804
57	Trinidad and Tobago	0.801

Medium human development

58	Libya	0.799
59	Republic of Macedonia	0.797
60	Antigua and Barbuda	0.797
61	Malaysia	0.796
62	Russian Federation	0.795
63	Brazil	0.792
64	Romania	0.792
65	Mauritius	0.791
66	Grenada	0.787
67	Belarus	0.786
68	Bosnia and Herzegovina	0.786
69	Colombia	0.785
70	Dominica	0.783
71	Oman	0.781
72	Albania	0.780
73	Thailand	0.778
74	Samoa	0.776
75	Venezuela	0.772
76	Saint Lucia	0.772
77	Saudi Arabia	0.772
78	Ukraine	0.766
79	Peru	0.762
80	Kazakhstan	0.761

81	Lebanon	0.759
82	Ecuador	0.759
83	Armenia	0.759
84	Philippines	0.758
85	China	0.755
86	Suriname	0.755
87	Saint Vincent and the Grenadines	0.755
88	Paraguay	0.755
89	Tunisia	0.753
90	Jordan	0.753
91	Belize	0.753
92	Fiji	0.752
93	Sri Lanka	0.751
94	Turkey	0.750
95	Dominican Republic	0.749
96	Maldives	0.745
97	Turkmenistan	0.738
98	Jamaica	0.738
99	Iran	0.736
100	Georgia	0.732
101	Azerbaijan	0.729
102	Palestine	0.729
103	Algeria	0.722
104	El Salvador	0.722
105	Cape Verde	0.721
106	Syria	0.721
107	Guyana	0.720
108	Viet Nam	0.704

109	Kyrgyzstan	0.702
110	Indonesia	0.697
111	Uzbekistan	0.694
112	Nicaragua	0.690
113	Bolivia	0.687
114	Mongolia	0.679
115	Moldova	0.671
116	Honduras	0.667
117	Guatemala	0.663
118	Vanuatu	0.659
119	Egypt	0.659
120	South Africa	0.658
121	Equatorial Guinea	0.655
122	Tajikistan	0.652
123	Gabon	0.635
124	Morocco	0.631
125	Namibia	0.627
126	São Tomé and Principe	0.604
127	India	0.602
128	Solomon Islands	0.594
129	Myanmar	0.578
130	Cambodia	0.571
131	Botswana	0.565
132	Comoros	0.547
133	Laos	0.545
134	Bhutan	0.536
135	Pakistan	0.527
136	Nepal	0.526

137	Papua New Guinea	0.523
138	Ghana	0.520
139	Bangladesh	0.520
140	Timor-Leste	0.513
141	Sudan	0.512
142	Congo	0.512
143	Togo	0.512
144	Uganda	0.508
145	Zimbabwe	0.505

Low human development

146	Madagascar	0.499
147	Swaziland	0.498
148	Cameroon	0.497
149	Lesotho	0.497
150	Djibouti	0.495
151	Yemen	0.489
152	Mauritania	0.477
153	Haiti	0.475
154	Kenya	0.474
155	Gambia	0.470
156	Guinea	0.466
157	Senegal	0.458
158	Nigeria	0.453
159	Rwanda	0.450
160	Angola	0.445
161	Eritrea	0.444
162	Benin	0.431
163	Côte d'Ivoire	0.420

164	Tanzania	0.418
165	Malawi	0.404
166	Zambia	0.394
167	Democratic Republic of the Congo	0.385
168	Mozambique	0.379
169	Burundi	0.378
170	Ethiopia	0.367
171	Central African Republic	0.355
172	Guinea-Bissau	0.348
173	Chad	0.341
174	Mali	0.333
175	Burkina Faso	0.317
176	Sierra Leone	0.298
177	Niger	0.281

Source: United Nations Development Programme Report 2005, [internet 21.10.2005]
http://hdr.undp.org/statistics/data/indic/indic_4_1_1.html

List of countries by income equality 2005

Rank	Country	Gini index	Richest 10% to poorest 10%	Richest 20% to poorest 20%	Survey year
1	Denmark	24.7	8.1	4.3	1997
2	Japan	24.9	4.5	3.4	1993
3	Sweden	25	6.2	4	2000
4	Belgium	25	7.8	4.5	1996
5	Czech Republic	25.4	5.2	3.5	1996
6	Norway	25.8	6.1	3.9	2000
7	Slovakia	25.8	6.7	4	1996
8	Bosnia and Herzegovina	26.2	5.4	3.8	2001
9	Uzbekistan	26.8	6.1	4	2000
10	Finland	26.9	5.6	3.8	2000
11	Hungary	26.9	5.5	3.8	2002
12	Republic of Macedonia	28.2	6.8	4.4	1998
13	Albania	28.2	5.9	4.1	2002
14	Germany	28.3	6.9	4.3	2000
15	Slovenia	28.4	5.9	3.9	1998
16	Rwanda	28.9	5.8	4	1983
17	Croatia	29	7.3	4.8	2001
18	Ukraine	29	6.4	4.3	1999
19	Austria	30	7.6	4.7	1997
20	Ethiopia	30	6.6	4.3	1999
21	Romania	30.3	8.1	5.2	2002
22	Mongolia	30.3	17.8	9.1	1998
23	Belarus	30.4	6.9	4.6	2000
24	Netherlands	30.9	9.2	5.1	1999
25	Russia	31	7.1	4.8	2002

26	South Korea	31.6	7.8	4.7	1998
27	Bangladesh	31.8	6.8	4.6	2000
28	Lithuania	31.9	7.9	5.1	2000
29	Bulgaria	31.9	9.9	5.8	2001
30	Kazakhstan	32.3	7.5	5.1	2003
31	Spain	32.5	9	5.4	1990
32	India	32.5	7.3	4.9	1999
33	Tajikistan	32.6	7.8	5.2	2003
34	France	32.7	9.1	5.6	1995
35	Pakistan	33	7.6	4.8	1998
36	Canada	33.1	10.1	5.8	1998
37	Switzerland	33.1	9.9	5.8	1992
38	Sri Lanka	33.2	8.1	5.1	1999
39	Burundi	33.3	19.3	9.5	1998
40	Yemen	33.4	8.6	5.6	1998
41	Latvia	33.6	9.2	5.6	1998
42	Poland	34.1	8.6	5.5	2002
43	Indonesia	34.3	7.8	5.2	2002
44	Egypt	34.4	8	5.1	1999
45	Kyrgyzstan	34.8	8.6	5.5	2002
46	Australia	35.2	12.5	7	1994
47	Algeria	35.3	9.6	6.1	1995
48	Greece	35.4	10	6.2	1998
49	Israel	35.5	11.7	6.4	1997
50	Ireland	35.9	9.7	6.1	1996
51	United Kingdom	36	13.8	7.2	1999
52	Italy	36	11.6	6.5	2000
53	New Zealand	36.2	12.5	6.8	1997

54	Jordan	36.4	9.1	5.9	1997
55	Azerbaijan	36.5	9.7	6	2001
56	Nepal	36.7	9.3	5.9	1995
57	Georgia	36.9	12	6.8	2001
58	Moldova	36.9	10.3	6.5	2002
59	Vietnam	37	9.4	6	2002
60	Laos	37	9.7	6	1997
61	Estonia	37.2	14.9	7.2	2000
62	Armenia	37.9	11.5	6.8	1998
63	Jamaica	37.9	11.4	6.9	2000
64	Tanzania	38.2	10.8	6.7	1993
65	Portugal	38.5	15	8	1997
66	Mauritania	39	12	7.4	2000
67	Morocco	39.5	11.7	7.2	1998
68	Mozambique	39.6	12.5	7.2	1996
69	Tunisia	39.8	13.4	7.9	2000
70	Turkey	40	13.3	7.7	2000
71	Trinidad and Tobago	40.3	14.4	8.3	1992
72	Guinea	40.3	12.3	7.3	1994
73	Cambodia	40.4	11.6	6.9	1997
74	United States	40.8	15.9	8.4	2000
75	Turkmenistan	40.8	12.3	7.7	1998
76	Ghana	40.8	14.1	8.4	1998
77	Senegal	41.3	12.8	7.5	1995
78	Singapore	42.5	17.7	9.7	1998
79	Kenya	42.5	13.6	8.2	1997
80	Iran	43	17.2	9.7	1998
81	Uganda	43	14.9	8.4	1999

82	Nicaragua	43.1	15.5	8.8	2001
83	Thailand	43.2	13.4	8.3	2000
84	Hong Kong (PR China)	43.4	17.8	9.7	1996
85	Ecuador	43.7	44.9	17.3	1998
86	Uruguay	44.6	18.9	10.4	2000
87	Cameroon	44.6	15.7	9.1	2001
88	Côte d'Ivoire	44.6	16.6	9.7	2002
89	People's Republic of China	44.7	18.4	10.7	2001
90	Bolivia	44.7	24.6	12.3	1999
91	Philippines	46.1	16.5	9.7	2000
92	Costa Rica	46.5	25.1	12.3	2000
93	Guinea-Bissau	47	19	10.3	1993
94	Dominican Republic	47.4	17.7	10.5	1998
95	Madagascar	47.5	19.2	11	2001
96	The Gambia	47.5	20.2	11.2	1998
97	Burkina Faso	48.2	26.2	13.6	1998
98	Venezuela	49.1	62.9	17.9	1998
99	Malaysia	49.2	22.1	12.4	1997
100	Peru	49.8	49.9	18.4	2000
101	Malawi	50.3	22.7	11.6	1997
102	Mali	50.5	23.1	12.2	1994
103	Niger	50.5	46	20.7	1995
104	Nigeria	50.6	24.9	12.8	1996
105	Papua New Guinea	50.9	23.8	12.6	1996
106	Argentina	52.2	39.1	18.1	2001
107	Zambia	52.6	41.8	17.2	1998
108	El Salvador	53.2	47.4	19.8	2000
109	Mexico	54.6	45	19.3	2000

110	Honduras	55	49.1	21.5	1999
111	Panama	56.4	62.3	24.7	2000
112	Zimbabwe	56.8	22	12	1995
113	Chile	57.1	40.6	18.7	2000
114	Colombia	57.6	57.8	22.9	1999
115	Paraguay	57.8	73.4	27.8	2002
116	South Africa	57.8	33.1	17.9	2000
117	Brazil	59.3	68	26.4	2001
118	Guatemala	59.9	55.1	24.4	2000
119	Swaziland	60.9	49.7	23.8	1994
120	Central African Republic	61.3	69.2	32.7	1993
121	Sierra Leone	62.9	87.2	57.6	1989
122	Botswana	63	77.6	31.5	1993
123	Lesotho	63.2	105	44.2	1995
124	Namibia	70.7	128.8	56.1	1993

Source: United Nations Development Programme Report 2005, [internet 21.10.2005]
http://hdr.undp.org/reports/global/2005/pdf/HDR05_HDI.pdf

—